anythink

MILITARY ENGINEERING
☆ ☆ ☆
IN ACTION

BIOSECURITY

PREVENTING BIOLOGICAL WARFARE

Earle Rice Jr.

E **Enslow Publishing**
101 W. 23rd Street
Suite 240
New York, NY 10011
USA

Published in 2017 by Enslow Publishing, LLC.
101 W. 23rd Street, Suite 240, New York, NY 10011

Library of Congress Cataloging-in-Publication Data

Names: Rice, Earle, author.
Title: Biosecurity : preventing biological warfare / Earle Rice Jr.
Other titles: Preventing biological warfare
Description: New York, NY : Enslow Publishing, [2017] | Series: Military engineering in action | Includes bibliographical references and index.
Identifiers: LCCN 2016010537| ISBN 9780766075436 (library bound) | ISBN 9780766075412 (pbk.) | ISBN 9780766075429 (6-pack)
Subjects: LCSH: Biological warfare—Juvenile literature. | Biological warfare—Prevention—Juvenile literature. | Biological weapons—Juvenile literature. | Bioterrorism—Prevention—Juvenile literature.
Classification: LCC UG447.8 .R45 2016 | DDC 358/.384—dc23
LC record available at http://lccn.loc.gov/2016010537

Printed in the United States of America

To Our Readers: We have done our best to make sure all website addresses in this book were active and appropriate when we went to press. However, the author and the publisher have no control over and assume no liability for the material available on those websites or on any websites they may link to. Any comments or suggestions can be sent by e-mail to customerservice@enslow.com.

Photos Credits: Cover, p. 1 Aaron Amat/Shutterstock.com (soldier in gas mask, p. 2), Davide Calabresi/ Shutterstock.com (ambulance); art/background throughout Dianka Pyzhova/Shutterstock.com, Ensuper/ Shutterstock.com, foxie/Shutterstock.com, kasha_malasha/Shutterstock.com, pashabop/Shutterstock. com; p. 4 Manny Ceneta/Stringer/Getty Images; p. 6 CHRIS KLEPONIS/Stringer/Getty Images; p. 7 FBI/Getty Images; p. 8 U.S. Department of Defense; p. 10 AP Photo/Frederick News Post, Sam Yu; p. 12 INA/Getty Images; p. 14 Douglas Graham/Congressional Quarterly/Getty Images; p. 15 Giorgio Rossi/Shutterstock. com; pp. 17, 21, 31, 37 © AP Images; p. 22 Tatiana Shepeleva/Shutterstock.com; p. 23 U.S. Air Force; p. 24 Sgt. Melissa Parrish/dvids; p. 25 U.S. Army; p. 28 Everett Historical/Shutterstock.com; p. 33 The Asahi Shimbun/Getty Images; p. 35 dvids; p. 39 ECBC Communications; p. 41 dikobraziy/Shutterstock.com; p. 42 Jezper/Shutterstock.com.

CONTENTS

The US Capitol was closed for a sweep for anthrax contamination after a suspicious letter was found in the office of the Senate majority leader.

Anthrax Panic

The first letters were mailed on September 18, 2001. It was one week to the day after terrorists attacked the World Trade Center towers in New York City and the Pentagon in Virginia. Across the nation, Americans were already emotionally shattered by the devastating attack by foreign terrorists on the US homeland. Five letters were postmarked with that date and a Trenton, New Jersey, postmark. Four were sent to the offices of ABC News, CBS News, NBC News, and the *New York Post*, all located in New York City. A fifth letter was sent to the *National Inquirer* at American Media, Inc. (AMI) in Boca Raton, Florida.

The letters contained anthrax spores. Anthrax is an infectious disease transmitted by a bacterium in warm-blooded animals. The powdery substance in the *Post* letter was described as a coarse brown granular material. Only the letters to NBC News and the *New York Post* were recovered. The existence of the other three was presumed because people at ABC, CBS, and AMI became infected.

Three weeks later, on October 9, two more letters were mailed. They bore the same Trenton postmark and contained highly refined powder consisting of almost pure anthrax spores. One was

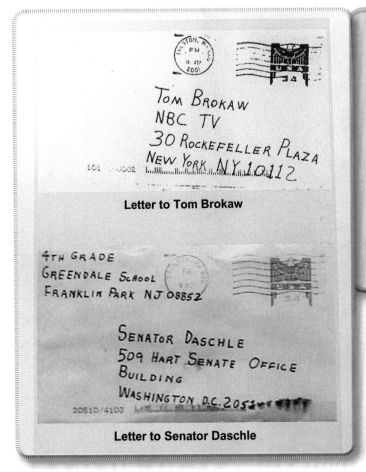

Letter to Tom Brokaw

Letter to Senator Daschle

Letters sent to NBC in New York and to the Washington, DC, office of US senator Tom Daschle contained anthrax bacteria. Both were postmarked in Trenton, New Jersey, and the handwriting on the envelopes matched.

addressed to Democratic senator and Senate Majority Leader Tom Daschle of South Dakota; the other, to Democratic senator and head of the Senate Judiciary Committee Patrick Leahy of Vermont. Neither of the two letters reached their addressees. An aide intercepted the letter to Daschle; the Leahy letter was rerouted by mistake to the State Department mail annex in Virginia.

On October 5, 2001, Robert Stevens of AMI died from inhaling anthrax (called inhalational anthrax). Over the next several weeks, four more people died from inhalational anthrax and seventeen others were sickened by the anthrax attacks. Most contracted infections were cutaneous (skin) infections.

Anthrax Letters

The letters received at NBC News and the *New York Post* contained photocopies of the same hand-printed threatening note. A similar photocopied note, crudely printed by the same hand, was enclosed in the letters sent to the two senators. Both versions of the note ended with the phrases "DEATH TO AMERICA/DEATH TO ISRAEL/ALLAH IS GREAT." The phrases were meant to suggest a link to the 9/11 terrorists. Fears of biological terrorism gripped the nation.

This is the letter that was sent to Senate Majority Leader Tom Daschle.

> 09-11-01
>
> YOU CAN NOT STOP US.
> WE HAVE THIS ANTHRAX.
> YOU DIE NOW.
> ARE YOU AFRAID?
> DEATH TO AMERICA.
> DEATH TO ISRAEL.
> ALLAH IS GREAT.

The FBI Investigates

Because the US mail was used and state lines were crossed to carry out the crimes, the Federal Bureau of Investigation (FBI) became immediately involved in the investigation. The FBI labeled the case "Amerithrax" and formed the Amerithrax Task Force of close to thirty investigators from several government agencies. The case would go on for the next nine years.

Owing to the sophisticated refinement of the anthrax spore, the FBI investigation quickly centered on the US Army Medical Research Institute of Infectious Diseases (USAMRIID) at Fort Detrick, Maryland.

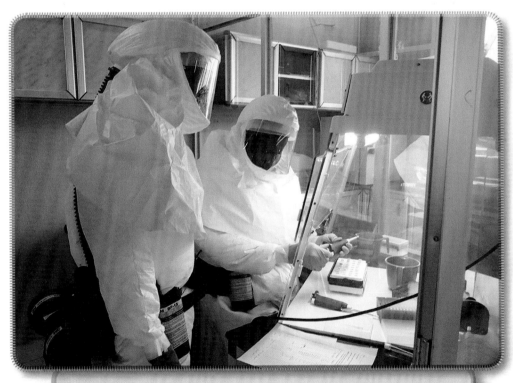

Technicians are suited up within a USAMRIID laboratory. Samples are handled in a negative-pressure biological safety cabinet to provide an additional layer of protection.

During a long, tedious investigation, the FBI eventually turned its attention to Bruce E. Ivins, a biodefense researcher at the institute.

Lab records at Fort Detrick showed that Ivins had logged dozens of late hours before the anthrax letter mailings. Further, a check into his background revealed clear indications of mental instability. For example, in a Department of Justice transcript of a secretly taped interview, Ivins implied he might have done things he could not remember. "I, in my right mind, wouldn't do it," he said of the anthrax attacks, adding, however, "It worries me when I wake up in the morning and I've got all my clothes and my shoes on, and my car keys are right there beside me."

In July 2008, Ivins learned that the FBI was about to press charges against him in connection with the anthrax attacks. As a possible motive, the *Los Angeles Times* reported that Ivins stood to profit "from massive federal spending in the fear-filled aftermath of those [anthrax] killings." Ivins held patents on anthrax and biodefense vaccines. Before charges were filed against him, Ivins took his own life by overdosing on acetaminophen (Tylenol). He died on August 29, 2008.

The Justice Department, the FBI, and the US Postal Inspection Service announced the formal conclusion of the Amerithrax investigation on February 19, 2010. According to the Justice Department report, "Evidence developed from that investigation established that Dr. Ivins, alone, mailed the anthrax letters." Some sources criticized the investigation and believe Ivins was innocent, but the case will likely remain forever closed.

The anthrax panic of 2001 awakened the nation to its vulnerability to biological attacks. To enhance its ability to deal with future investigations, the FBI created the Weapons of Mass Destruction Directorate (WMDD) in July 2006. Its creation, according to an FBI science briefing, "is another example of the FBI's progressive approach focusing on prevention as well as investigation of all issues involving chemical, biological, radiological, and nuclear materials." The WMDD plays an important role in the nation's biosecurity.

Bruce E. Ivins was the scientist who was developing a vaccine to combat anthrax. After seven years of probing the deadly 2001 anthrax mailings, the FBI formally closed the case, concluding that the government researcher acted alone.

Biosecurity

Biosecurity has many meanings. Various scientific disciplines define it differently. The National Academies of Science define biosecurity as "security against the inadvertent, inappropriate, or intentional malicious or malevolent use of potentially dangerous biological agents or biotechnology, including the development, production, stockpiling, or use of biological weapons as well as outbreaks of newly emergent and epidemic disease." Closely related terms are *biodefense, biowarfare,* and *bioterrorism.* Their definitions are defined by the Journal of *Bioterrorism and Biodefense* as follows:

Biodefense "refers to short term, local, usually military measures to restore biosecurity to a given group of persons in a given area who are, or may be, subject to biological warfare—in the civilian terminology, it is a very robust biohazard response."

Biowarfare "is the use of biological toxins of infectious agents such as bacteria, viruses, and fungi with the intent to kill or incapacitate humans, animals, or plants as an act of war." It is also called g*erm warfare*.

Bioterrorism "is terrorism involving the intentional release or dissemination of biological agents like bacteria, viruses, or toxins, and may be in a naturally occurring or a human-modified form." The anthrax attacks represent a prime example of bioterrorism.

Iraqi president Saddam Hussein practices launching a rocket-propelled grenade during the Iraq-Iran War.

CHAPTER 2

Biowarfare Through the Ages

"Together we must also confront the new hazards of chemical and biological weapons and the outlaw states, terrorists, and organized criminals seeking to acquire them." So spoke President Bill Clinton in his State of the Union address to the US Congress on January 27, 1988—three years before the start of the Gulf War of 1991. He went on to say, "Saddam Hussein has spent the better part of this decade and much of his nation's wealth not on providing for the Iraqi people, but on developing nuclear, chemical, and biological weapons, and the missiles to deliver them."

President Clinton was right in warning the nation's leaders about the hazards of biological weapons, but they are far from being new weapons. In the case of biological weapons, it truly can be said that there is nothing new under the sun.

President Clinton speaks during his January 1998 State of the Union address at the Capitol.

Not to Worry

A Department of Homeland Security (DHS) bulletin issued in 2011 stated: "Over the last decade, violent extremists have expressed aspirational interest in contaminating unspecified water supplies, and as recently as July 2011 specifically raised backpressure as a means of contamination."

"Backpressure happens when there is a pressure, higher than the city water pressure, exerted on the water systems and it causes the water to flow backward," explained Roy Dillard, in an article on the DHS website.

Backpressure commonly occurs when a water main breaks. Anything in that line would get siphoned into the main line. Using backpressure, terrorists might introduce chemical or biological agents into the water supply and spread it over long distances long before its detection.

"It's possible," Dillard said. "Virtually any kid taking a high school science class could figure it out, but it would have to be done in such volumes that it would be relatively hard to do because . . . we use backflow prevention assemblies in major areas and in almost all of your industrial areas."

All fifty states require controlled cross-connections and backflow prevention systems. Even if terrorists tried to inject a biological agent into a water supply, chlorine in the tap water would likely nullify it. "Our water systems are pretty well protected," Dillard said.

Backpressure can occur after a water main pipe breaks.

Evolving Bioterror Methods

As early as 600 BCE, armies recognized the potential impact of infectious diseases on opposing armies as well as on the civilian population. Combatants would often pollute wells and other water sources of their enemies with human corpses, animal carcasses, and other filth. Assyrians used rye ergot to poison the wells of their enemies. Ergot is a fungus that grows on rye and produces a drug similar to LSD. Those who consumed the ergot-infected water became ill or died. The use of such crude methods continued right into the twentieth century.

As late as medieval times, people had yet to understand how germs spread disease. From the 1100s through the 1600s, medical professionals believed the foul odor from decaying bodies was the means by which disease was circulated. But then as now, their actions were guided by whatever worked—and their coarse attempts at biological warfare worked.

Moving into the 1700s, Russian troops catapulted plague-infected bodies into Swedish cities during the Great Northern War (1710–1721). British soldiers distributed blankets from smallpox victims to Native Americans in the French-Indian War (1754–1767). In one such incident, according to a Texas Department of State Health Services History of Bioterrorism, smallpox-laden blankets were passed to two members of the Delaware tribe. William Trent, a local militia commander, later noted in his journal: "Out of our regard for them, we gave them two Blankets and a Handkerchief out of the Small Pox Hospital. I hope it will have the desired effect." And in 1797, no less a historical figure than Napoleon Bonaparte himself flooded the plains around Mantua, Italy, in hopes of enhancing the spread of malaria during the siege of an Austrian army post.

During the US Civil War (1861–1865), Confederate agents—improvising on a well-tested tactic from earlier war fighters—sold clothing from yellow fever and smallpox patients to Union troops.

See Something, Say Something

Since the 9/11 terrorist attacks, experts and ordinary citizens alike have thought a time or two about the possibility of a terrorist attack on America's agriculture. According to Stephen Goldsmith, a veterinarian with the FBI's Biological Countermeasures Unit, a so-called agroterrorism event is possible but highly unlikely. Goldsmith used foot-and-mouth disease as an example. If the disease is detected, it would shut down the export of every live or processed food or other product at once. And access to American livestock is openly available.

Goldsmith has recommended stepping up biosecurity. Steps include using gate and door locks, monitoring livestock for unusual clinical symptoms, screening and training new employees, and watching for strangers or unusual happenings in the area.

"We don't want you to lay awake at night, get nervous and have ulcers, but think about things," he said. Americans should stay vigilant and say something to police or other authorities, if they see something suspicious.

These cattle are being raised in pens at a feedlot in Nebraska. Livestock are potential targets of agroterrorism.

In World War I, Germany shipped anthrax-infected cattle to the United States and other countries. And the Japanese experimented with biological warfare in occupied-Manchuria around 1936.

World War II and Beyond

Numerous incidents of biowarfare occurred during World War II (1939–1945). In China, the Japanese dropped bags of plague-infested fleas and grains on cities. Japanese forces contaminated wells and distributed poisoned foods in China. Allied scientists experimented with biological agents but did not use them against their enemies.

The United States established the USAMRIID in 1969 (see chapter 5) to advance its defenses against biological warfare. Today, the institute continues to work at the cutting edge of America's biological defenses.

During the Iraq-Iran War (1980–1988), Iraq's oppressed Kurdish minority sided with the Iranians. On March 17, 1988, the whine of jet engines shattered the predawn stillness in the Iraqi foothills near Iran. A wave of Iraqi—Soviet-built—MiG fighter-bombers swept across the frost-covered hills and dropped a combination of antipersonnel cluster bombs and nerve-gas missiles on the Kurdish city of Halabja. The warheads contained various lethal agents, most notably the nerve gases sarin and VX. Twenty MiG bombing runs across the city left some five thousand Kurds dead and another twenty thousand severely wounded.

The atrocity was directed by Iraqi dictator Saddam Hussein. After the Gulf War of 1991, his representatives revealed to members of the UN Special Commissions Team 7 that Iraq had experimented with anthrax, botulinum toxins, and food-poisoning bacteria. Saddam's use of chemical warfare, and his admitted attempts to add biological warfare to his weapons of mass destruction (WMD) arsenal, would contribute to his end a decade later.

Bioterror, Bioagents, and Biosurveillance

"**W**e lived with that fear on a daily basis," Sue Proffitt told Gillian Flaccus of the Associated Press (AP), seventeen years after the event. "We understand in The Dalles how bioterrorism can happen." Proffitt was a clerk in Wasco County, Oregon, and one of the victims when cultists terrorized the county and the city of The Dalles in 1984.

The first call to the Wasco County Health Department came on September 17, 1984. A resident of The Dalles reported a case of food poisoning after dining at a restaurant in town. It was the first of many such calls from diners in local restaurants. Within a week of the outbreak, the Centers for Disease Control and Prevention (CDC) determined the cause as *Salmonella typhimurium*. The bacterium eventually infected some 750 people in the town of 10,000.

In the early 1980s, a gray-bearded guru calling himself Bhagwan Shree Rajneesh arrived in New York City from India. (*Bhagwan* is Hindi for "god.") He soon migrated to Oregon and bought a one-hundred-square-mile site once known as the Big Muddy ranch. There Rajneesh formed a commune of followers. Dressed in red and wearing beaded necklaces with picture pendants of their leader, they became known as Rajneeshees.

Initially, citizens of the nearest town of Antelope accepted their presence with a live-and-let-live attitude. Neighbors grew concerned, though, as they watched the Rajneeshees build a small city in an area that was legally designated as farmlands. The burgeoning city included not only roads, dairy barns, and greenhouses, but also cafeterias, hotels, and medical clinics. Local concerns turned to alarm when the red-garbed Rajneeshees began attending town council meetings in nearby Antelope in an effort to gain political power. But the Rajneeshees were just getting started.

Determined to seize political control of Wasco County, cult leaders began busing in homeless people to expand their commune and thus their voting power. When that was not enough to sway elections their way, the Rajneeshees realized that they somehow had to keep opposition voters from the polling booths. They turned to germ warfare.

The Rajneeshees planned to contaminate the county water supply with *Salmonella* bacteria cultivated in their own medical laboratories. To test its potency, they laced the salad bars in The Dalles with their homemade germs. One restaurant owner later said he lost $465,000 in sales and liability claims from infected customers.

During the following months, citizens of the county lived in fear over concerns that cult members might poison the water or spread the AIDS virus. "People were so horrified and so scared," Laura Bentley told the AP. "People wouldn't go out, they wouldn't go out alone. People were becoming prisoners."

Fortunately for the good people of Wasco County, the Rajneesh cult collapsed under federal investigation and prosecution in

Cult leader Bhagwan Shree Rajneesh, right, speaks with his disciples in Oregon. Patrons of ten restaurants in The Dalles, Oregon, became ill in September 1984 after being poisoned by members of the religious cult who sprayed lab-cultured *Salmonella* bacteria onto salad bars over a two-week period.

1985. Some cult members were imprisoned, others deported. Rajneesh himself was fined $400,000 for immigration fraud and was deported. And the largest ever attack of bioterrorism on US soil ended.

Bioagents

According to the US Department of Health and Human Services (HHS), *Salmonella* bacteria cause 1.2 million illnesses, 23,000 hospitalizations, and 450 deaths each year. The CDC separates *Salmonella* and other bioterrorism agents into three categories:

Category A organisms or toxins pose the greatest public health and national security risks: They can easily be spread from person to person; result in high death rates; might cause major health impacts, public panic, and disruption; and require special action for health preparedness.

Category B agents are fairly easy to spread; result in moderate illness rates and low death rates; and need special laboratory enhancements and enhanced disease monitoring.

Category C includes new pathogens (infectious agents) that might later be prepared for mass spread. They are readily available, are easy to produce, and have the potential for major health impact, including high disease and death rates.

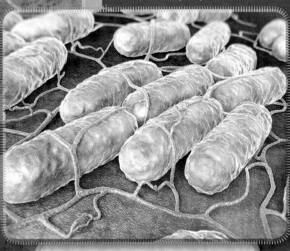

Salmonella bacteria, shown magnified, are a CDC Category B agent.

Biosurveillance and Biosafety

In the late 1990s, scientists from the US Department of Defense (DoD) began to focus on the development and use of vaccines for biodefenses. A 2001 DoD report listed vaccines considered to be "DoD-critical products." Listed were vaccines against anthrax, smallpox, plague, tularemia, botulinum, ricin, and equine encephalitis.

Defense against biowarfare and bioterrorism targets two distinct populations: civilian noncombatants and military combatants (troops in the field). A critical part of civilian defense requires protection of water sources and food supplies. Defending combat

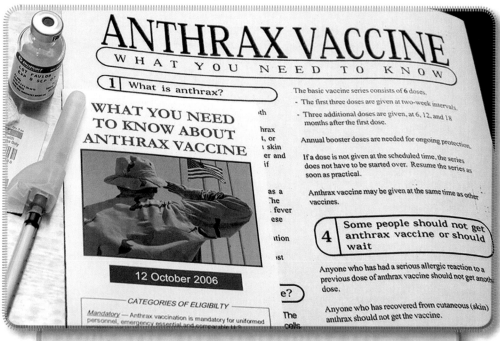

An anthrax vaccine brochure is available for military personnel to review prior to receiving their vaccination. The Anthrax Vaccine Immunization Program mandates personnel assigned to high-threat areas to receive the anthrax vaccine series.

FACT

Marching On!

France's great military leader Napoleon Bonaparte once said, "An army marches on its stomach." Imagine what would happen if an army's enemy contaminated its food supply. At the very least, it would cripple the army's ability to operate. That is why protection of the Department of Defense's food and water supplies is a major function of the US Army Public Health Command (USAPHC).

"The primary focus of food defense is the prevention of the intentional contamination of our food supply, while food safety is aimed at preventing unintentional or accidental contamination," explained Sgt. 1st Class Kevin M. Gill, in an article by Jane Gervasoni on army.mil.

"Although food safety had been a mainstay of Army veterinary food inspectors, food defense had not even been a focus of discussion until after September 11, 2001," added Col. Thomas E. Honadel, USAPHC Veterinary Services Food Protection Program manager. "Since that time, more emphasis has been placed on antiterrorism food defense plans."

"Food defense measures include training for food service personnel, increased security of food service areas, and even background and identification checks," Gill continued. Personnel like Gill and Honadel protect the food supplies of the US Army.

US Army captain Sarah Anne Simpson, health protection officer for Multinational Battle Group-East, inspects the bread making process with the owner of a Kosovo bakery.

Gone Gobblers

In November 2013, a shipment of Thanksgiving food arrived at Camp Bondsteel in Kosovo. It contained an abundance of turkeys for a holiday feast for the American troops stationed there. It fell to Staff Sgt. Kimberly Kornaki to inspect the shipment and verify that it was protected from contamination during transit. Kornaki was a member of the US Army Public Health Command (USAPHC), deployed with Task Force Medical Falcon.

"I knew there was a problem as soon as I checked the truck with the food shipment and found brown cylindrical pellets on the floor of the vehicle and on top of the food," Kornaki said. "Checking for contamination is an important part of the inspection process, and what I saw raised a red flag." She rejected the shipment, which effectively canceled Thanksgiving dinner for the troops. The gobblers were gone.

A later examination of the food shipment found no contamination. Officials arranged a replacement shipment, and the troops celebrated Thanksgiving a few days late. Staff superiors commended Kornaki for doing the right thing. "The support my force health team receives in Kosovo is truly amazing," she said. "I am just happy being able to contribute to the mission in Kosovo."

When Staff Sgt. Kimberly Kornaki inspected a food truck delivery destined for consumption by military service members and their families on Thanksgiving, she noticed brown pellets on the floor and on top of the packages. She rejected the shipment.

troops against bioweapons relies heavily on protective clothing and gear and vaccinations.

Before and during the Gulf War (1990–1991), coalition forces anticipated the enemy's potential use of biological and chemical weapons. They trained in protective masks and equipment, practiced decontamination procedures, and received extensive instructions on detection and immunization methods. About 150,000 US troops were vaccinated against anthrax, and another 8,000 received a new botulinum vaccine.

In the civil defense sector, experts recognize biosurveillance as the single most important tool for identifying public health events of worldwide significance. Emerging infectious diseases reside high on the list.

Biosurveillance consists of four basic functions: 1) detect and report disease within a given population; 2) analyze and confirm reported cases to detect outbreaks; 3) respond quickly and appropriately at the local or regional levels to prevent and control disease outbreaks at the national level; and 4) provide information on the causes, distribution, and control of diseases in populations.

Currently, there are at least twenty-nine biosurveillance systems on constant alert in the United States to help ensure the biosafety of all Americans.

Dark Winter

It was 2001. Winter came early that year. It came to Oklahoma City, Philadelphia, and Atlanta in June. And the winter was dark and threatening. Rather than a reversal of seasons, it was a kind of modern-day morality play. It was aptly called Dark Winter. Its cast of characters consisted of seventeen top-level government employees, public servants, and members of the news media. Government officials came from assorted departments and agencies—Defense, Justice, State, Health and Human Services, Federal Emergency Management Agency, FBI, and CIA.

The "winter" began on June 22 in an indoor amphitheater at Andrews Air Force Base (now Joint Base Andrews) outside Washington, DC. With the cast assembled around a table centered in the pit, according to Chuck Staresinic in *PITTMED*, the national security adviser said, "Before we begin this evening, I think it is important that you see what is currently on the local TV station in Oklahoma City...This was taped from a live broadcast about 15 minutes ago."

Smallpox

Through the ages, smallpox claimed the lives of more people in Europe than the plague. It killed some 300 million people in the twentieth century alone. Smallpox is caused by the variola virus that emerged in ancient times. It was finally eradicated from the earth by a worldwide vaccination program. The last case of smallpox in the United States occurred in 1947. Somalia recorded the last naturally occurring case in the world in 1979. But both the United States and Russia still retain small quantities of the smallpox virus in laboratories in Atlanta and Koltsovo, respectively.

Smallpox is a serious, contagious, infectious disease. It appears in two clinical forms: variola major and variola minor. Smallpox can be passed from one person to another by prolonged face-to-face contact. It can also be spread through direct contact with infected bodily fluids or contaminated objects such as clothing or bedding. Spread of the virus in the air is rare but possible in closed settings such as buildings, buses, and trains.

Smallpox is characterized by fever, followed by a rash of variable severity that blisters, dries up, and leaves scars. Variola major is fatal about 30 percent of the time; variola minor is much less severe, with a fatality rate of less than 1 percent.

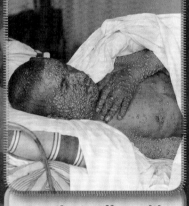

A patient suffers with smallpox in Palestine in the early 1900s.

The eyes of every cast member turned to focus on a large screen. A female television newscaster in Oklahoma City was staring into the camera and informing her audience about "an outbreak of a mystery sickness." The camera cut to a male journalist who reported that at least five patients at a local hospital might have smallpox. "Now that's a deadly virus not seen in this country for at least 20 years," he said, "so if it proves true, we could have a serious health emergency on our hands." Tensions heightened at the meeting as visions of a biological scourge danced eerily in the minds of the viewers.

Adding to the mounting fears, the president announced that the CDC had confirmed the presence of as many as twenty cases of smallpox in Oklahoma City. "A large proportion of the world population is now susceptible to smallpox," he said. "If this situation is not handled correctly, we could be facing the beginning of a nationwide or global epidemic."

Oklahoma Governor Frank Keating was among the officials at the table. At the suggestion of a potential epidemic, he immediately sought assurances that all of Oklahoma's 3.5 million residents would receive the smallpox vaccine within the next seventy-two hours. His request posed a problem: Only 12 million doses existed in a nation of some 280 million people. If a third of the available vaccine was used in one state, what would happen if the outbreak spread to other states? That question was about to be answered.

Alarming Answers

An update of the situation a few hours later reported twenty confirmed cases of smallpox in Oklahoma City. Another fourteen were suspected. Further reports indicated nine suspected cases in Pennsylvania and seven in Georgia. The CDC confirmed that there was indeed an outbreak of smallpox. Over the next thirteen days, the disease spread to twenty-five states and fifteen countries. Its source remained unknown.

Five Key Findings

The Dark Winter simulation yielded five key findings about the US health care system's ability to cope with a bioterrorism attack.

- A biological attack on the United States would threaten vital national security interests.
- Existing organizations lacked the structure and capability to efficiently manage a biological attack.
- Neither the US health care and public health systems nor the drug and vaccine industries possessed an adequate capability to deal with mass casualties.
- Dealing with the media would present a major challenge to all levels of government in the management of both a crisis and its consequences.
- Significant ethical, political, cultural, operational, and legal challenges would arise from the use of a contagious bioweapon infectious agent.

At the same time, a US carrier task force was deployed to the Middle East amid an emerging threat to national security. Adding to the mix, tensions were rising in the Taiwan Straits. Government officials at Andrews appeared to have a full-blown national emergency on their hands. But all is not always as it seems.

Dark Winter was a simulated event designed to test America's preparedness for a biological attack on the US homeland. Participants at Andrews focused on the public health response and an inadequate supply of vaccine. They examined the roles and responsibilities of federal and state governments, and the impact

Drills for responding to an actual bioterrorism event are an important part of training. Here, Hazmat Response Unit members, dressed in protective gear, walk fictitiously contaminated UCLA workers into a decontamination shower. The drill was part of the county's bioterrorism preparedness exercise.

on social liberties related to quarantine and isolation. Lastly, they looked at the role of the DoD and how the military would respond to an anonymous attack. The entire operation played out under the 24/7 scrutiny of the news media.

In real life, the results of the exercise foretold a genuine "dark winter."

Alarmed by the findings of Dark Winter, then-president George W. Bush ordered the manufacture of 300 million doses of smallpox vaccine. Additionally, between 2001 and 2011, the federal government spent more than $60 billion to heighten America's biodefense. Upgrades consisted of developing and distributing air sensors, teaching doctors how to recognize symptoms of bioagents, and distributing medical supplies for biodefense throughout the nation.

Combatting Biological Threats

Bioterror and toxin attacks pose a constant threat not only to the United States but also to the world at large. On March 20, 1995, the Japanese cult Aum Shinrikyo ("Supreme Truth") carried out a toxic attack in Japan's subway system using the nerve agent sarin. During the morning rush hour, cult members stashed packages containing a liquid form of sarin onto five cars in three separate lines that converged at a Tokyo station. The cultists punctured the packages, which looked like lunch boxes or bottled drinks, and left them to leak.

When the trains pulled into the station, frantic passengers jammed the subway entrance. Most lay gasping on the ground and bleeding from their noses and mouths. Twelve victims died and an estimated six thousand more sought medical attention.

Passengers rescued from the subway station lie on the ground at Tokyo Metro Kayabacho Station on March 20, 1995, in Tokyo, Japan. The chemical terrorist attack by Japanese doomsday cult Aum Shinrikyo happened at almost the same time on five subway lines during the morning commuter peak hours, killing twelve people.

Shoko Asahara, the founder of Aum Shinrikyo, was convicted and sentenced to death. Twelve other Aum members are on death row.

Hiroyuki Nagaoka, the father of a former Aum member, explained the mindset of the Aum cult members to staff writer Masamiito of the *Japan Times*: "Aum turned our children into mindless people without a sense of their own free will. They became unable to determine good from bad and that is why Aum members didn't think twice about murder. They became Asahara's puppets."

In today's twenty-first-century world, countless terrorist organizations exist with similar collective mindsets. Groups like the Islamic State (ISIS, or ISIL), Al Qaeda, and many others hold no qualms about killing those who do not share their beliefs. Their existence demands that all free nations mount a constant and vigorous biodefense. The US Army Medical Research Institute of Infectious Diseases (USAMRIID) stands at the forefront of America's defense against bioterrorists.

Biodefense Vanguard

USAMRIID, located at Fort Detrick, Maryland, specializes in research on biological threats. Its primary job is to provide medical solutions for the protection of service members, but its expertise can also be used to protect the entire population as needed by developing medical solutions—vaccines, drugs, diagnostics, and information—to bioterror threats. It is the only Department of Defense (DoD) laboratory equipped to safely study highly hazardous infectious agents that require maximum containment at Biosafety Level 4 (BSL-4). A biosafety level is the level of containment needed to work with a given biological agent. It is based on the risk posed by the agent and the activities involved with the testing. Scientists at USAMRIID strive every day to maintain the laboratory's world-class scientific and technology base.

USAMRIID is a national laboratory. It—and other laboratories like it—represent the key elements of the Laboratory Response Network (LRN). In addition to its primary work to protect military troops, USAMRIID's scientists provide expert consultation and training for medical personnel. LRN laboratories are responsible for characterizing specialized strains, bioforensics, and handling highly infectious biological agents. Such work requires much planning, as well as state-of-the-art facilities for the safety and security of the scientists.

At USAMRIID, most LRN testing is done in laboratories equipped for Biosafety Level 3, but it is one of only a few US laboratories with

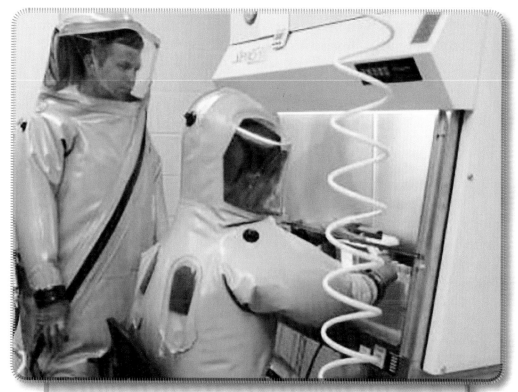

Ebola virus research is conducted in maximum containment Biosafety Level 4, or BSL-4, laboratories, where investigators wear positive-pressure suits and breathe filtered air while they work.

BSL-4 facilities. Each biosafety level requires its own set of safety equipment, facilities, and practices to reduce the risk of getting infected in the laboratory. Personnel working in BSL-4 laboratories, for example, must wear full-body pressurized suits that resemble the space suits worn by astronauts. The suits provide the highest form of personal protective equipment. Those who work in BSL-4 labs must also take chemical showers, then enter a vacuum room to be exposed to ultraviolet light. This process destroys any trace amounts of the organisms after testing.

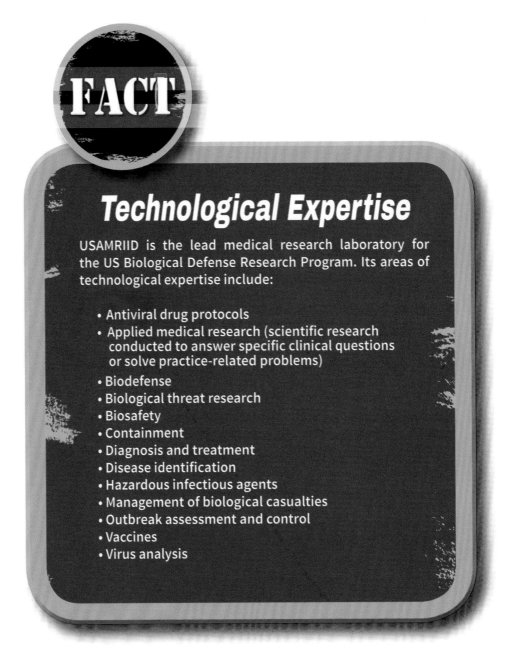

Technological Expertise

USAMRIID is the lead medical research laboratory for the US Biological Defense Research Program. Its areas of technological expertise include:

- Antiviral drug protocols
- Applied medical research (scientific research conducted to answer specific clinical questions or solve practice-related problems)
- Biodefense
- Biological threat research
- Biosafety
- Containment
- Diagnosis and treatment
- Disease identification
- Hazardous infectious agents
- Management of biological casualties
- Outbreak assessment and control
- Vaccines
- Virus analysis

Biological Warfare Training

The training of worldwide first responders is high on the list of the services provided by USAMRIID. First responders include hazardous materials teams, National Guard Support Teams, tactical response teams, emergency communications, and others. USAMRIID's Field Operations and Training (FO&T) Branch offers two first-responder courses: Biological Agent Identification and Counterterrorism Training (BAIT) and Field Identification of Biological Warfare Agents (FIBWA).

The FIBWA program consists of four different core courses: 1) Basic Course, 2) Manager's Course, 3) National Guard Bureau & Civil Support Teams, and 4) Special Interest Training. The program runs for twenty working days. Students learn to set up, maintain, and operate mobile laboratories under field conditions for both biowarfare and biosurveillance missions. Emphasis is placed on using a combination of several technologies. These lessons are

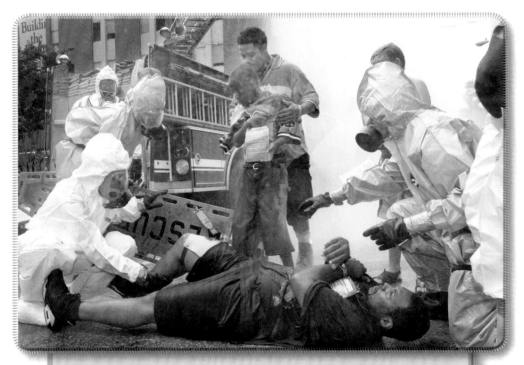

Emergency personnel in chemical and biological protective suits respond to the simulated injuries of a victim who has just passed through a decontamination shower. Emergency training exercises held by the US Air Force simulate a terrorist attack.

FACT

BAIT

The Biological Agent Identification and Counterterrorism Training (BAIT) is one of several courses offered by USAMRIID. It teaches responders to be prepared for biological threats. Experts stage customized scenarios for single organizations or several at once. The staff then monitors and reviews training operations with responders after completion. As listed on USAMRIID's website, BAIT provides:

- Realistic integrated training for responders to bioterrorism events
- True subject matter experts for recommending improvements to organizational functions
- CD/USB recording of exercise
- Realistic biowarfare samples
- Multiple day exercises with biowarfare refresher training
- Mobile Training Teams

coupled with "hands-on" laboratory experience aimed at reaching a highly reliable solution.

Americans can rest a little easier knowing that the USAMRIID stands at the vanguard of America's defense against a full range of biological threats—both on the battlefield and on the domestic front.

Video Games, Anyone?

Personnel at the US Army Edgewood Chemical Biological Center (ECBC) are working hard to give soldiers a "leg up" in combating chemical biological attacks.

ECBC, part of the US Army Research, Development and Engineering Command, employs a staff of 1,400 civilians and two military personnel. Sgt. Maj. Jamison L. Johnson serves as senior enlisted advisor to the director. "Coming here as a noncommissioned officer," Johnson said, in an interview with Martha C. Koester for *NCO Journal*, "I realized right away what the capabilities were here and how much this place has to offer. It's quite amazing."

"The engineers, the product developers, the warfighters, we are integrated so . . . we [can] start using this technology in a specific way to do training for Chemical, Biological, Radiological, Nuclear and Explosives (CBRNE) missions," explained Jeffrey A. Warwick, conceptual modeling and animation team leader. "It's great to train soldiers on the things they need to recognize and learn."

Team members with backgrounds in computer science, art, and animation develop multimedia and interactive training aids for soldiers. They use video game technology and virtual reality headsets to create realistic programs for training soldiers for CBRNE missions. Training the ECBC way can be effective, fun, and *amazing*!

Edgewood Chemical Biological Center military Deputy Colonel Debra Daniels tries out a virtual reality head-mounted display.

Imminent Threats

In the mid-1300s, the bubonic plague killed 60 percent of the European population. The plague was commonly known as the Black Death. It caused huge boils on its victims, who then suffered a slow, painful death. In today's exciting—but dangerous—times many might wonder what would happen if terrorists got their hands on the plague to use as a weapon of biowarfare. With the rise of terrorist groups such as the Islamic State (ISIS), the threat of such a happening has become increasingly more imminent.

"It could happen in the near future because of how they are changing the face of terrorism and it's changing at an alarming rate," said terrorism expert Chris Ryan, speaking with Sam Webb of the UK newspaper *Express*. "They're trying to come up with different ways to kill people and also how to shock people. It's a real possibility."

In an August 2014 article in *Foreign Policy*, Harald Doornbos and Jenan Moussa detailed further evidence of deadly terrorist intent.

A laptop computer belonging to an IS terrorist named Muhammed S. was recently found in Syria. It contained a nineteen-page primer in Arabic on developing biological weapons and weaponizing the bubonic plague from infectious animals. It said in part: "The advantage of biological weapons is that they do not cost a lot of money, while human casualties can be huge."

The nineteen-page document went on with instructions on how to achieve the best results with a viral weapon: "Use small grenades with the virus, and throw them in closed areas like metros [subways], soccer stadiums, or entertainment centers. Best to do it next to air-conditioning. It can also be used during suicide operations." It left little doubt as to the evil aspirations of the terrorists.

In 2014, Islamic terrorists seized about a third of the land in both Iraq and Syria and established the Islamic State. Many terrorism experts agree that the longer they control the land as a base of operations the more imminent the threat of a bioterror event will become. Some observers believe IS technologists are already at work developing bioweapons in the Iraqi city of Mosul or the Syrian city of Raqqa.

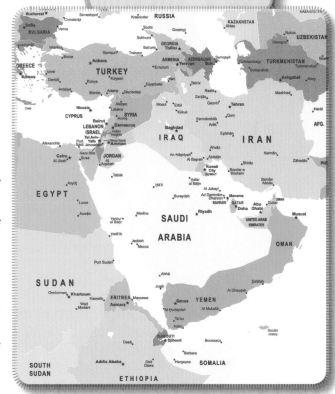

ISIS militants have seized areas in Iraq and Syria.

Black Biology

The dangers of bioterror threats are clear and present. They are increased not only by the possibility of bioweapons use by terrorists, but also by the advances of modern molecular biology. Each scientific and technological advance increases the potential more sophisticated bioweapons.

The dark practice of using modern techniques in molecular biology to create advanced varieties of bioweapons is known as "black biology." Scientists are currently developing techniques to improve the effectiveness of bioweapons. Paraphrased from a listing by Mackenzie Foley, in *Applied Sciences*, they include:

- **Binary biological weapons**—Harmless microbes combined with deoxyribonucleic acid (DNA) to increase toxicity within the host bacteria.
- **Designer genes**—Pathogens designed by creating synthetic genes (molecular units of heredity), viruses, and possibly entirely new organisms.
- **Gene therapy**—Replacement of existing genes with harmful genes.
- **Stealth viruses**—Viral infections that enter the cells of a human host and remain dormant until triggered.
- **Host-swapping diseases**—Genetically modified animal viruses developed to infect humans.
- **Designer diseases**—Cellular mechanisms manipulated to cause diseases.

A computer model shows the double helix structure of DNA.

Biowarfare Prevention

For most people, few things can be more frightening than the intentional contamination of life-sustaining necessities—air, water, or food supplies—by bioterrorists. World leaders recognized the dangers of germ warfare shortly after World War I. In 1925, they signed the Geneva Protocol prohibiting the use of chemical and biological weapons in war. A half-century later, the provisions of the Geneva Protocol were supplemented by those of the 1972 Biological and Toxic Weapons Convention (BWC).

The BWC took effect in 1975. By the turn of the century, some 144 nations had signed onto it. Additional provisions and legislations have been proposed to control bioweapons. So far, the United States has declined to adopt them. American leaders have expressed fear that some of the new proposals might reveal vital US military secrets and thus pose a threat to national security. Failure of safeguards to keep pace with biological advances pleads the question of how the world can defend against evolving bioweapons.

Many methods are needed to defend against existing and evolving forms of bioweapons. High on the list is continual improvement of and stricter adherence to existing international conventions banning WMDs. Some militants suggest the use of nuclear retaliation to deter bioterrorists. Perhaps the best biodefense resides with emerging tools of genetic knowledge and biological technology. These include immune system enhancement, new vaccines, antibiotics and antiviral drugs, and efficient bio-agent detection and identification equipment.

Most importantly for Americans, the US government needs to actively pursue methods of biodefense to protect its citizens. "Unfortunately, biological threats are not given the same level of attention as are other threats, leaving us significantly unprepared," said former senator Joe Lieberman, in a press release noted by Kevin Loria in *Tech Insider*. "[B]ut this does not have to be the case."

There is no better time than now to alter the case.

Bioweapons Convention

The 1972 Biological and Toxin Weapons Convention (BWC) was the first international treaty to ban an entire class of weapons. Article I of the BWC, as noted by the Federation of American Scientists, reads as follows:

Each state party to this Convention undertakes never in any circumstances to develop, produce, stockpile or otherwise retain: (1) Microbial or other biological agents, or toxins whatever their origin or method of production, of types and in quantities that have no justification for prophylactic [disease preventative], protective or other peaceful purposes; (2) Weapons, equipment or means of delivery designed to use such agents or toxins for hostile purposes or armed conflict.

The BWC treaty includes additional articles to ensure continued international cooperation and agreed-upon implementation of its provisions.

TIMELINE

1300—Bubonic plague kills 60 percent of the European population.

1754–1767—British soldiers distribute blankets from smallpox victims to Native Americans in the French-Indian War.

1984—Rajneeshees contaminate salad bars in The Dalles, Oregon, with *Salmonella typhimurium*.

1988—Iraq drops a combination of antipersonnel cluster bombs and nerve-gas missiles on the Kurdish city of Halabja.

1995—Japanese cult Aum Shinrikyo carries out a toxic attack against Japan's subway system using the nerve agent sarin.

1998—President Bill Clinton warns the nation about the new hazards of chemical and biological weapons.

2001—Anthrax letters kill five people and sicken seventeen others. Dark Winter exercise reveals America's unpreparedness for a biological attack.

2006—FBI creates the Weapons of Mass Destruction Directorate.

2008—Dr. Bruce E. Ivins, suspected originator of the anthrax letters, commits suicide.

2010—FBI formally closes Amerithrax investigation.

2014—Islamic State is founded in Iraq and Syria. Laptop computer is found with documents revealing biowarfare aspirations of terrorists.

2015—Terrorism expert Chris Ryan warns of future bioterrorist attacks.

allegation—Statement made without proof.

assessment—An estimate of the worth, quality, or likelihood of a given entity.

bacterium—A microscopic organism.

contaminate—To pollute.

deployable—Capable of being spread out, utilized, or arranged.

immunization—The act of making a human or animal immune, that is, resistant to infection.

inoculate—To treat a person or animal with vaccines or serums, etc., especially to prevent diseases.

malevolent—Something productive of harm or evil.

morality play—Something that involves a direct conflict between right and wrong or good and evil from which a moral lesson may be drawn.

parasite—An animal or plant that lives on or in another from which it draws its nourishment.

quarantine—Isolation imposed on people or animals that may have been exposed to an infectious or contagious disease that they could spread to others.

scenario—A sequence of events; an account or synopsis of a possible course of action or events.

sophisticated—Highly complicated or developed.

susceptible—Without resistance; open to infection.

weapon of mass destruction (WMD)—A chemical, biological, or radiological weapon capable of causing widespread death and destruction.

FURTHER READING

BOOKS

Currie-McGhee, Leanne K. *Bioethics*. 1st ed. eBook. Farmington Hills, MI: Lucent Books, 2009.

Marcovitz, Hal. *Biological & Chemical Warfare*. Edina, MN: Abdo Publishing, 2010.

Nardo, Don. *Invisible Weapons: The Science of Biological and Chemical Warfare*. North Mankato, MN: Compass Point Books, 2011.

Robson, Hal David. *Weapons and Defense Research*. San Diego, CA: Reference Point Press, 2012.

WEBSITES

Biological Warfare
encyclopedia.kids.net.au/page/bi/Biological_warfare
Learn about the history, prevention, and technology of biological warfare.

Global Biodefense
globalbiodefense.com/
Read biodefense headlines, and news on pathogens and preparedness.

University of Illinois at Chicago: Germ Warfare/Biological Weapons
uic.edu/classes/osci/osci590/7_1Germ%20Warfare%20Biological%20 Weapons.htm
Read about germ warfare and biological weapons.

INDEX